Snowy

By Alice K. Flanagan

Snowflakes drift down from the sky. They land and collect on the ground. What a pretty sight!

Snow falls in a forest.

Winter clouds form in the sky.

Snow is frozen **moisture**. But how does snow form? Tiny drops of water in the air gather together and form clouds.

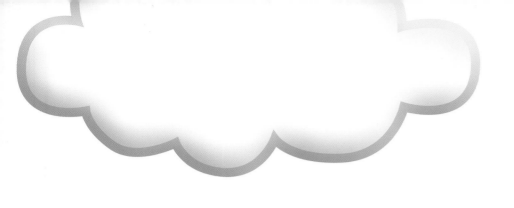

When it is cold, the drops of water turn into **ice crystals**. These crystals become too heavy to stay in the air. Then they fall as snowflakes.

The first snowfall of the winter covers the ground.

Snowflakes come in many shapes and sizes.

Snowflakes are not all the same size. Most are about the size of a pencil eraser. But some can be bigger than a quarter.

Most snowflakes have six sides. No two snowflakes look the same. Snow is clear, too. It just looks white when the light hits it.

Sunlight bounces off the snow.

It rarely snows in hot places such as Arizona.

Snow usually falls during the cold winter months. Some places do not get snow at all. The temperature there is too hot for ice crystals to form.

Snow acts like a blanket for the ground. It keeps plant roots safe from the wind and the cold. Snow keeps **burrowing** animals warm and dry.

A gopher stays warm by burrowing under snow.

Snow from a blizzard covers two bison.

Sometimes a snowfall can turn into a storm. This is called a **blizzard**.

When snow melts, it fills rivers and lakes. Animals and people can then use the water.

Melting snow drips into a stream.

Be sure to dress in warm clothes to play in the snow!

Snow can be light and fluffy or wet and sticky. Have fun when you play in the snow!

Glossary

blizzard (BLIZ-urd): A blizzard is a big snowstorm. A blizzard brings lots of snow.

burrowing (BUR-oh-ing): Burrowing means something is digging a hole in the ground to live. Burrowing animals stay warm under snow.

ice crystals (EYSS KRISS-tuls): Ice crystals are water that freezes in certain shapes. Ice crystals can form in clouds.

moisture (MOYS-chur): Moisture is a small amount of water. Frozen moisture forms snow.

To Find Out More

Books

Cassino, Mark. *The Story of Snow: The Science of Winter's Wonder*. San Francisco, CA: Chronicle Books, 2017.

Rylant, Cynthia. *Snow*. Boston, MA: Houghton Mifflin Harcourt, 2017.

Shaw, Gina. *Curious About Snow*. New York, NY: Grosset And Dunlap, 2016.

Websites

Visit our website for links about snow:
childsworld.com/links

Note to Parents, Teachers, and Librarians: We routinely verify our Web links to make sure they are safe and active sites. So encourage your readers to check them out!

Index

About the Author

Alice K. Flanagan lives with her husband in Chicago, Illinois, and writes books for children and teachers. Today, she has more than 70 books published on a wide variety of topics, from U.S. presidents to the weather.

The Child's World®
childsworld.com

Published by The Child's World®
1980 Lookout Drive • Mankato, MN 56003-1705
800-599-READ • www.childsworld.com

Photo credits: David B. Petersen/Shutterstock.com: 12; Gerald Bernard/Shutterstock.com: 4; Green Mountain Exposure/Shutterstock.com: 16; Juro Kovacik/Shutterstock.com: 19; MNStudio/Shutterstock.com: cover, 1; moosehenderson/Shutterstock.com: 15; Nickolay Khoroshkov/Shutterstock.com: 11; Scharfsinn/Shutterstock.com: 7; Sunny Forest/Shutterstock.com: 3; Triff/Shutterstock.com: 8; zlikovec/Shutterstock.com: 20

ISBN Hardcover: 9781503827905
ISBN Paperback: 9781622434589
LCCN: 2018939777

Printed in the United States of America • PA02398